G000162932

Color, Cut, Play Dress Paper Dolls

With this fashion activity book you can feel like a fashion designer.

For adults, paper dolls may be a gateway to childhood memories but they also make great gifts for children. While cutting out will improve their scissor skills, coloring the lineart can help finding good color combinations and developing a sense of style and design. Younger children may need help to cut these dolls out since the dolls and clothes are not perforated. However, this is a nice opportunity for fun family time. Paper dolls can bring adults and children together, and collections of paper dolls have always passed down to younger generations. New generations can learn a lot while playing with paper dolls. In a digital era where dress up games allow us to change clothes on paper dolls by only touching a screen, cutting these dolls the traditional way is a great help for developing motor skills. Playing together also helps to develop communication and cooperation between friends and family. Playing games goes hand in hand with storytelling, role-playing and fantasy so everyone can treasure the time spent playing with these paper dolls as memories full of creativity and imagination.

Paper dolls have a long history, and although inspired by antique and vintage paper dolls, these are modern fashion dolls.
Collecting these paper dolls and sharing them with children can also make fashion and design become one of their passions.

As an illustrator with a background in fashion design,
I had hours of fun drawing these paper dolls.
I really hope that paper doll fans and children of all ages
enjoy these creations as much as I did.
I wish everyone who is cutting out these dolls and trying the outfits
has a great time with this entertaining activity.

by
Basak Tinli

Color, Cut, Play Dress Up Color, Cut, Play Dress Up

by
Basak Tinli

Color, Cut, Play Dress Up Color, Cut, Play Dress Up

by Başak Tinli

by
Başak Tinli

Color, Cut, Play Dress Up Color, Cut, Play Dress Up
Color, Cut, Play Dress Up Color, Cut, Play Dress Up
Color, Cut, Play Dress Up Color, Cut, Play Dress Up
Color, Cut, Play Dress Up Color, Cut, Play Dress Up
Color, Cut, Play Dress Up Color, Cut, Play Dress Up
Color, Cut, Play Dress Up Color, Cut, Play Dress Up
Color, Cut, Play Dress Up Color, Cut, Play Dress Up

by
Başak Tinli

by Basak Tinli

Color, Cut, Play Dress Up
by Başak Tinli

Color, Cut, Play Dress Up
by Başak Tinli

by
Başak Tinli

Color, Cut, Play Dress Up
by Basak Tinli

Color, Cut, Play Dress Up Color, Cut, Play Dress Up

by Başak Tinli

Color, Cut, Play Dress Up
by Başak Tinli

by
Basak Tinli

by Başak Tinli

by
Başak Tinli

Color, Cut, Play Dress Up

Color, Cut, Play Dress Up
by Basak Tinli

Color, Cut, Play Dress Up
by Basak Tinli

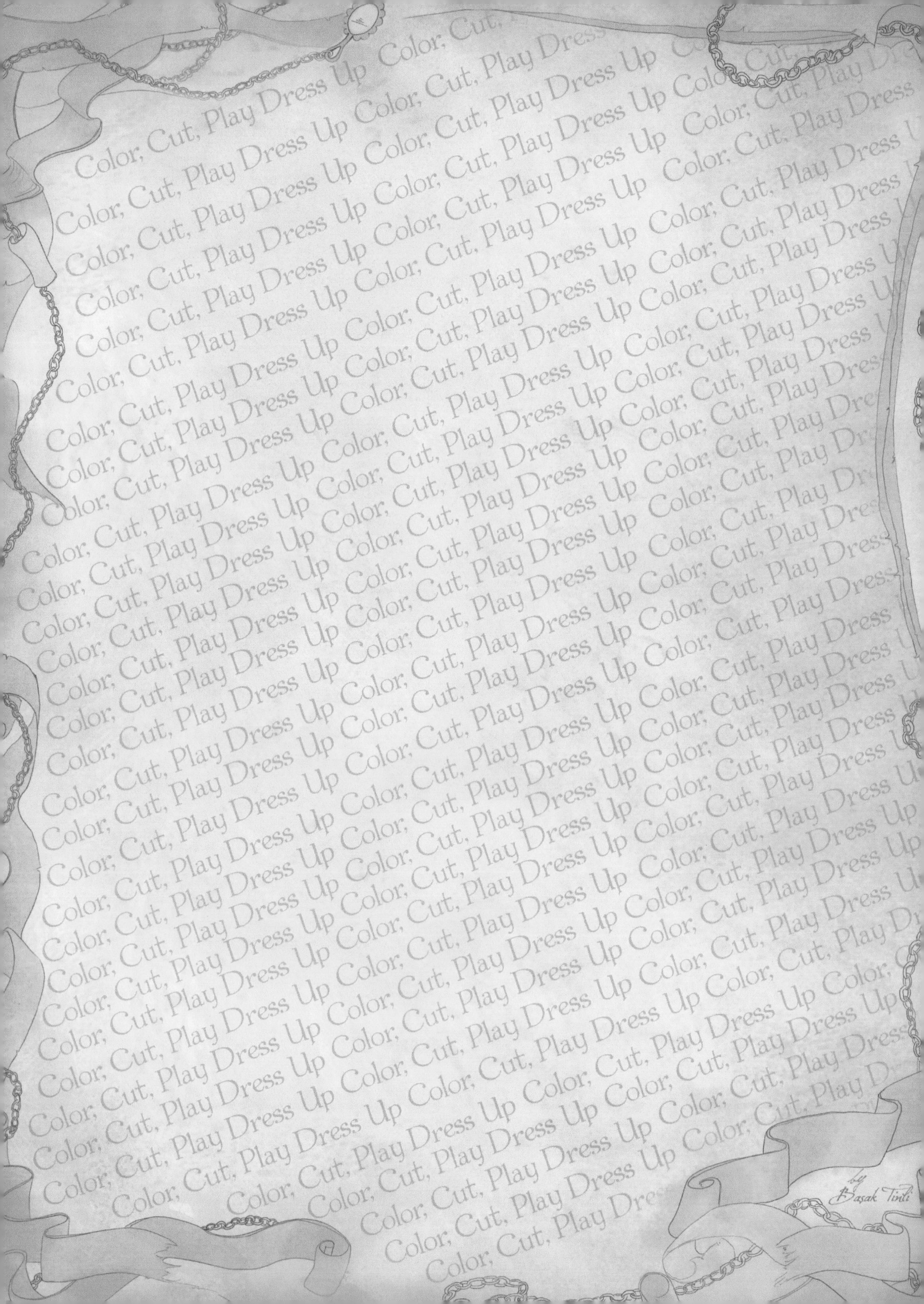
Color, Cut, Play Dress Up
by Basak Tinli

by Başak Tinli

by Başak Tinli

Color, Cut, Play Dress Up Color, Cut, Play Dress Up Color, Cut, Play Dress Up
Color, Cut, Play Dress Up Color, Cut, Play Dress Up Color, Cut, Play Dress Up
Color, Cut, Play Dress Up Color, Cut, Play Dress Up Color, Cut, Play Dress Up
Color, Cut, Play Dress Up Color, Cut, Play Dress Up Color, Cut, Play Dress Up
Color, Cut, Play Dress Up Color, Cut, Play Dress Up Color, Cut, Play Dress Up
Color, Cut, Play Dress Up Color, Cut, Play Dress Up Color, Cut, Play Dress Up
Color, Cut, Play Dress Up Color, Cut, Play Dress Up Color, Cut, Play Dress Up
Color, Cut, Play Dress Up Color, Cut, Play Dress Up Color, Cut, Play Dress
Color, Cut, Play Dress Up Color, Cut, Play Dress Up Color, Cut, Play Dress
Color, Cut, Play Dress Up Color, Cut, Play Dress Up Color, Cut, Play Dress
Color, Cut, Play Dress Up Color, Cut, Play Dress Up Color, Cut, Play Dress
Color, Cut, Play Dress Up Color, Cut, Play Dress Up Color, Cut, Play Dress
Color, Cut, Play Dress Up Color, Cut, Play Dress Up Color, Cut, Play Dress
Color, Cut, Play Dress Up Color, Cut, Play Dress Up Color, Cut, Play Dress
Color, Cut, Play Dress Up Color, Cut, Play Dress Up Color, Cut, Play Dress
Color, Cut, Play Dress Up Color, Cut, Play Dress Up Color, Cut, Play Dress Up
Color, Cut, Play Dress Up Color, Cut, Play Dress Up Color, Cut, Play Dress Up
Color, Cut, Play Dress Up Color, Cut, Play Dress Up Color, Cut, Play Dress Up
Color, Cut, Play Dress Up Color, Cut, Play Dress Up Color, Cut, Play Dress Up

by
Başak Tinli

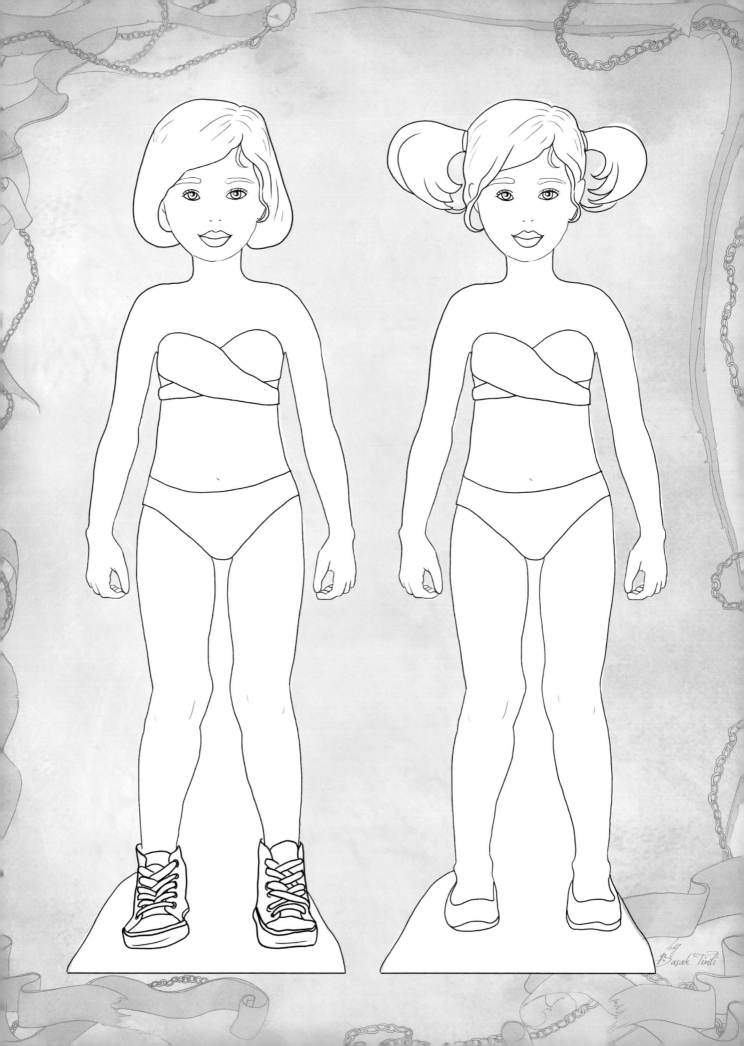

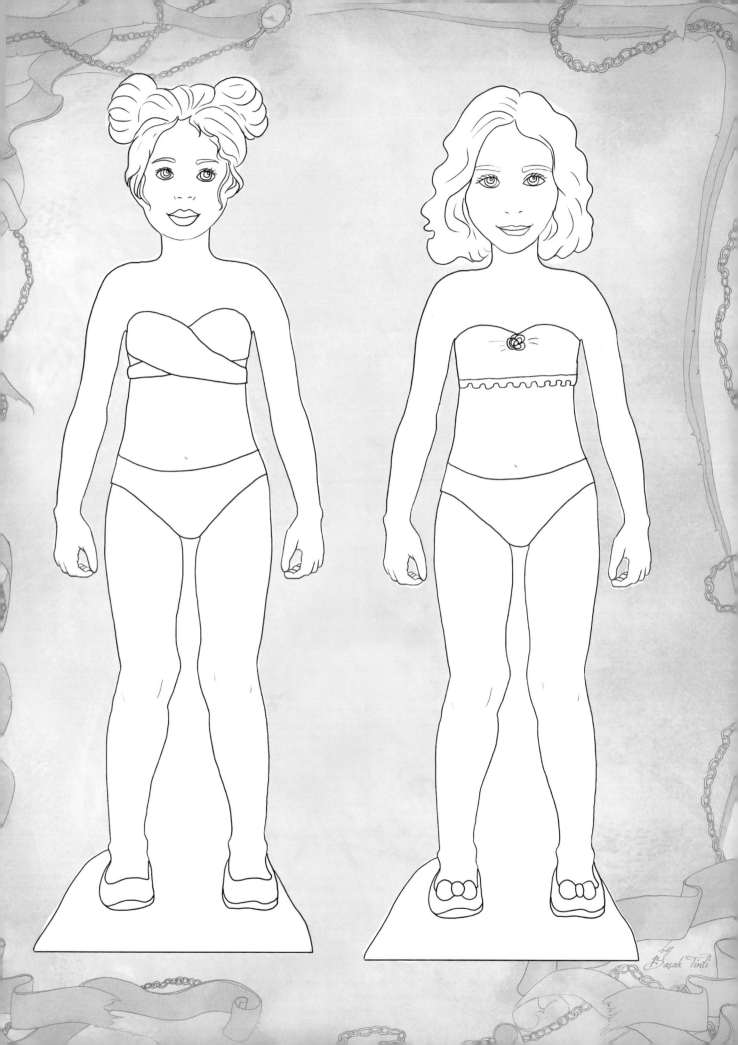

Color, Cut, Play Dress Up Color, Cut, Play Dress Up Color, Cut, Play Dress Up Color, Cut, Play Dress Up (repeated)

by Başak Tinli

Printed in Great Britain
by Amazon

79307118R00025